Midnight Musings

Mikayla Vittallo

BookLeaf Publishing

India | USA | UK

Presentation by *BookLeaf Publishing*

Web: www.bookleafpub.com

E-mail: info@bookleafpub.com

ISBN: 9789360944841

First edition 2024

To those that struggle in their own ways but keep seeing the next sunrise.

To my English teachers who saw the internal conflict well before anyone else did.

ACKNOWLEDGEMENT

Thank you to those that have read my work - both published and WIPs - your encouragement, love, and support while I take on this journey will forever have a place in my heart.

Thank you to Tia, who had to sit through the lore of each poem and still managed to make me laugh even as we connect red strings to new poems.

Thank you to Amy, who supported me and pushed me to make connections. Without your guidance I wouldn't have one of these poems and I wouldn't have realized that I wanted to release more books.

PREFACE

These poems deal with trauma in multiple forms, please take caution while reading.
Take time to practice self-care while reading.

12:43 AM

I once thought that
I would shatter over a
pebble.
That I was the thinnest pane of glass
But,
maybe that isn't the right
analogy.
Maybe,
    I'm a dandelion-
changing and growing to become
New.
A symbol of
      Resilience.

1:10 AM

Growing is the slowest
process
I have ever known.
I see no results anytime I look
and
then

I'm so far
away
from
where
I

       started.

1:27 AM

Fear holds me in a gilded cage.
The key is in my hands, yet,
I'm unable to leave.
Hands shaking, I try again.
This time I'll free myself,
from my own mind.

1: 37 AM

Always wishing to go home,
to a place I've never known.
I am wearing the familiar clothes
of a loved one,
yet, on me
everything is distorted.
The sweater,
once green,
is blue.
And the warmth,
normally comforting,
makes crawling out of
my skin
appealing.

1:40 AM

I have died so many times,
yet I walk.
      "you're annoying."
      "you talk sooo much."
      "can't you be still for a minute, please."
      "you're too much to handle."
      "I can't deal with you,
        when you're like this."

My heart, my passions, and so
much of me has crumpled
   in defeat
at the words of others,
and
the cruelest killer, from
myself.

1: 42 AM

i formed my whole
self
on what others wanted me
to be
and when i fell short
(Fall off that tight rope)
there was no end to the guilt.
(Until remorse took its place.)

1:56 AM

It's climbing its way up the walls.
It grows larger than what can be handled
alone.
I want to scream for help, but
my voice breaks.
it grows. You walk away.
It grows. My life seems to shrink.
The echos of me are being drowned
by what's inside this house.

2:00 AM

I'm not sure who I am,
a stranger in my body.
In this life,
there are growing pains,
learning-
> relearning-
myself
but there is more too,
hope.
> laughter.
>> love.

2:01 AM

Every actor has their role,
And I must perform mine,
Even on days,
I wish
to be free from this
stage.

2:19 AM

Sometimes when I say
  "I don't know"
what I mean is
     " Everything seems to be wrong and
     it is all-consuming, stopping the words
     in my throat until I manage to choke
     out   that   small   phrase. "

Sometimes when I say
  "I don't know"
what I mean is
     " My whole body is numb, but not in a
     physical way, I mean all my emotions
     are fuzzy, nothing is wrong I just can't
     feel like I used to. Sometimes I like it,
     sometimes   I   don't. "

i don't know.

2:30 AM

When dreams are too big
that I'm positive they would
take over the sky,
I work harder
to turn that into a reality.
Even if the sky is always
and forever more
Pink.

2:41 AM

those whispers in your head
are lies.
your fears will pass in time.
Please,
raise your head and
do not drown in those dark waters.
You will be a
survivor.

2:47 AM

I know the results
will be worth the journey.
But,
healing is a downward climb
up a mountain.
I'm struggling to pull myself
together.
How can I even admit that
I'm so
b r
   o
     k e
       n ?

2:55 AM

Anger,
is what holds me
together.
I feel that without
the tight grasp,
I would fall apart.
Shattered.
a family is supposed
to be there
for each other.
Yet, all you did was
leave me,
to fight alone.
I was shattered without
your shield.
I wish you realized your own
fault as I lay
bleeding.

3:15 AM

There's peace in the
woods
where fairytales live.
A witch's hut,
    created from a leaning branch.
A stone bridge,
    built where the rocks make a path.

My imagination
    and freedom
created magic
in those woods,
or maybe
the magic was there
to make me feel
        alive.

3: 19 AM

I want a life
of fairytales,
and
happily-ever-afters.
to be swept off my feet
with warmth and
love that I have
never known.
To be my own self,
while loved from
another person.

4:18 AM

I wish someone looked
at me
the way
I looked at the stars and sunrise.
And
I wish,
when they did that

I believed it.

4:29 AM

As the seasons change
   and summer sweeps in
memories filter in
 on the wind,
  as smoke.
I can hear my young laughter
and I realize why
I always
want to be
somewhere
   warm.

4:40 AM

I wonder if I run
headfirst into harm
or
does it seek me out?
trusting one's gut is only
for someone
whose never been
wrong.

I have found solace
in a viper's den,
how would
the kiss of a
lamb
compare?

5:16 AM

I wish I could tell you,
how terrified I am that
I have given too much of myself
out to the world,
to you,
that there is nothing
left for me.
I am so scared that
  I am
nothing.

5:55 AM

I was told that life
gets better
with time.
that darkness isn't
absolute.
And I scoffed,
this person, she-
who read my inner thoughts-
couldn't possibly understand.
Now,
years have passed and
sitting with joy in my lap,
surrounded by the mess
of sadness,
I wonder, if I was the one
who didn't
Understand.